How Your Pet Grows!

Caper the Kid

Jane Burton

Random House 🏠 New York

Library of Congress Cataloging in Publication Data: Burton, Jane. Caper the kid/by Jane Burton. (How your pet grows!) SUMMARY: Photographs and text follow two young pygmy goats as they grow, learn, and play during their first year of life. 1. Goats—Juvenile literature. 2. Pygmy goat—Juvenile literature. 3. Goats—Development—Juvenile literature. [1. Pygmy goat. 2. Goats.] I. Title. II. Series. SF383.35.B87 1988 636.3′07—dc19 88-6485 ISBN: 0-394-89962-8 (pbk.); 0-394-99962-2 (lib. bdg.)

Manufactured in Hong Kong 1 2 3 4 5 6 7 8 9 0

With thanks to Jennifer Spooner for all her help

Newborn twins Caper and Cap are just a few hours old. Their mother, Disco, licked them clean and dry. Then she gave them a drink of her milk. Now the baby goats, called "kids," are sleepy. They curl up together for a nap.

Each kid has a white "cap" on his head. Caper has white socks above his hoofs and a white patch on his belly like an apron.

Two days old

The twins were born knowing how to jump and climb. Like wild goats that live on steep, rocky mountains, Caper and Cap have hoofs that keep them from slipping.

Caper thinks that Disco makes a perfect mountain! He hops onto her back when she lies down. But as soon as she moves, he topples off. Now it is Cap's turn to balance on Disco's back. He will tumble off, too, if Disco moves.

One week old

One warm, sunny day the kids go outside. They romp happily around the field. Then Caper spots a gap in the fence and slips into the woods.

Caper explores for a while, but soon he feels lost. His loud bleats seem to say "I want my mother!" Disco answers him, and he dashes back to her. In the barn again, both kids begin to suckle. Drinking Disco's warm milk makes them feel safe and happy again.

One month old

Disco's friend Daisy has a kid named Daffodil who is the same age as Caper and Cap. The three kids run off and play together. When they return to their mothers, Daisy and Disco can tell which babies are theirs by sniffing them. Cap knows which nanny goat is *his* mother by the smell of her beard.

Inca, another goat, is in the field with her curly-coated kid. Caper joins them for a snack at the straw bale.

Llamas share the field with the goats.
Lizzie, the white llama, and Micha, who is
brown, come to feed. The kids perch on
top of the bale, so the big animals have to
eat from the sides.

Cap can leap up onto Disco's back—even
when she is standing! He is very surefooted
now and doesn't fall off when Disco walks
around.

Three months old

The twins are old enough to leave their mother. They move to their own little house under the shade of some big trees. Both kids

have grown little horns, which are very handy for scratching themselves and butting each other. Now they are wearing collars. Cap's is blue, and Caper's is red.

The kids are best friends.
Wherever Cap goes, Caper follows.
They love to race around their
house, kicking out and butting
each other in fun. They even eat
out of the same bowl without
fighting.

Four months old

Young goats are dainty feeders. They nibble a leaf here and a daisy there. They bite off a few twigs and munch a little mouthful of grass. They will eat almost anything—paper, string, people's clothes—but only if it is clean.

When they are full, they rest awhile. The food they have just eaten, called "cud," comes back up, one mouthful at a time. They chew it carefully and swallow it again. This helps their stomachs break up the tough leaves and grass.

Six months old

One night a terrible storm begins to blow. Sheets of rain batter the goathouse. The wind bellows and roars. With every blast, the little house rattles. Inside, the kids huddle together, trembling with fear.

The storm snaps branches from trees and hurls them through the air. Whole trees crash down in the woods, torn up by their roots.

Suddenly the kids hear a loud *crack!* and a *thud!* The roof of the goathouse crashes in, but the walls stand firm.

In the morning the house is hidden beneath a tangle of tree limbs. The twins look out at a strange new world.

Caper and Cap tiptoe nervously out of their house. A big tree has fallen and broken the fence around their field. There are leafy branches lying everywhere. The kids sniff some leaves and then take a bite.

The kids hop over the broken fence and begin to explore. Soon they come to a paved road. There are no cars around because fallen trees are blocking the road.

The pavement under their hoofs feels like rock to Caper and Cap. They prance around excitedly and kick their heels in the air. They even butt heads just for fun!

Jack the dog is out for a walk. He sees that
Caper and Cap have gotten out of their
field. Jack is a border collie and knows what
to do when animals are straying. He runs
around and around the two little goats,
trying to drive them home.

But Caper and Cap do not want to be
herded along like two meek little lambs.
While Jack runs around them, they spin
and face him with their horns. Jack rushes
bravely at Caper, barking to turn him. But
Caper rears up and then butts Jack on the
side with his head.

Poor Jack! He was only trying to help!

Seven months old

The fence is still broken, so Caper and Cap
set off on another adventure. This time
they go into the woods, where the autumn
leaves have started to fall and cover the
ground.

Later the goats meet some big ducks.
Caper goes over to sniff the nearest one.
But the ducks squawk angrily and waddle
away.

Eight months old

The kids have lots of places to climb now. Their favorite spot is the big tree that fell onto their house during the storm. They hop along its huge trunk, nibbling twigs and leaves as they go.

Cap is more daring than Caper. He climbs higher and walks right to the sawed edge of the fallen tree. Caper peers up at him, perched high in the air like a wild goat on a mountain peak.

Ten months old

It is midwinter now. The goathouse and the fence have been repaired at last. Even though the kids' horns are still small and their beards have just sprouted, Caper and Cap are nearly full grown. The twins will stay together for the rest of their lives. Each night they will curl up, side by side, just like they did when they were first born.